Building Essential Vocabulary

Reproducible Photo Cards, Games, and Activities to Build Vocabulary in Any Language

by
Sherrill B. Flora

illustrations by
Julie Anderson

Publisher
Key Education Publishing Company, Ll
Minneapolis, Minnesota

D1451322

CONGRATULATIONS ON YOUR PURCHASE OF A KEY EDUCATION PRODUCT!

The editors at Key Education are former teachers who bring experience, enthusiasm, and quality to each and every product. Thousands of teachers have looked to the staff at Key Education for new and innovative resources to make their work more enjoyable and rewarding. Key Education is committed to developing and publishing educational materials that will assist teachers in building a strong and developmentally appropriate curriculum for young children.

PLAN FOR GREAT TEACHING EXPERIENCES WHEN YOU USE EDUCATIONAL MATERIALS FROM KEY EDUCATION PUBLISHING COMPANY, LLC.

Credits
Author: Sherrill B. Flora
Editor: George C. Flora
Cover Design: Mary Claire
Inside Illustrations: Julie Anderson
Photography: © Banana Stock
　　　　　　© Brand X
　　　　　　© Comstock
　　　　　　© Corbis
　　　　　　© InDesign
　　　　　　© Ingram
　　　　　　© PhotoDisc
　　　　　　© Rubberball
　　　　　　© Vivid

Key Education welcomes manuscripts and product ideas from teachers.
For a copy of our submission guidelines, please send a self-addressed, stamped envelope to:

Key Education Publishing Company, LLC
Acquisitions Department
9601 Newton Avenue South
Minneapolis, Minnesota 55431

Standard Book Number: 1-9033052-12-0
Building Essential Vocabulary
Copyright © 2005 Key Education Publishing Company, LLC
Minneapolis, Minnesota 55431

Introduction

Educators that work with young children are experiencing a significant increase in the number of English language learners enrolled in their classrooms. The United States census estimates that there are approximately 13 million children from preschool through age 18 who do not speak English as their first language. These children represent over 400 different languages spoken in today's schools. In the last ten years, the number of students learning English as a new language in the United States has increased by seventy-two percent and nearly half of all teachers in public schools now teach at least one student with limited proficiency in English.

As a result of this incredible increase, teachers are in need of targeted resource materials that promote language development and assist in quickly building vocabulary. *Building Essential Vocabulary* is an easy-to-use resource that provides teachers with over 400 reproducible photo cards, games, and activities that can be used to **teach vocabulary in any language**. The cards and games can be inexpensively reproduced and used for classroom "English" activities, while additional photo card sets can be copied and sent home with the children.

It has been well documented that children who are exposed to two languages at an early age—and simultaneously—will naturally learn both languages with fewer speech and language problems. Sending home duplicate sets of photo cards, games, and activities will provide parents with tools for increasing "home" language skills and, at the same time, reinforce what the children have learned at school. Research has also shown that it is easier for children to learn a second language while they are actively learning a first language.

As educators, we have learned that the best way for children to increase language skills and build vocabulary is to use realistic photographs, concrete objects, and to have the children work on increasing their vocabulary through fun and non-threatening activities. Some of the most successful language experiences can happen through the playing of games and practicing language in meaningful context.

All the activities provided in *Building Essential Vocabulary* are effective for all children, whether they are learning a first, second, or even a third language. The photo cards, games, and activities were designed to provide exciting, entertaining, and purposeful experiences that will help build the vocabulary that is required for effective communication.

Contents

Unit 1: Animals
Farm Animals, Pets, and Wild Animals

1. **REPRODUCIBLE PHOTO CARDS** are found on pages 6 and 7. *(English and Spanish Vocabulary Lists can be found on page 90.)*

PHOTO CARDS:

(Farm & Pets, page 6)

1. cat	5. fish	9. mouse
2. cow	6. hamster	10. pig
3. dog	7. hen	11. rabbit
4. duck	8. horse	12. sheep

(Wild Animals, page 7)

13. alligator	17. leopard	21. shark
14. elephant	18. lion	22. snake
15. giraffe	19. monkey	23. tiger
16. hippopotomus	20. rhinoceros	24. zebra

2. **BINGO, LOTTO, AND MEMORY MATCH GAMES** can easily be created with the photo cards. Use the reproducible Lotto game board *(page 88)* and the Bingo game card *(page 89)* to make the games. Complete directions for all three games are found on page 87.

3. **REPRODUCIBLE PAGES:** Directions for **Down on the Farm** *(page 8)* and **The Pet Store** *(page 9)* are found on each specific page.

4. **MUSIC:** Children learn quickly with rhythm and rhyme. The songs "Old McDonald," "I'm Going to the Zoo," "The Farmer in the Dell," and "How Much is That Doggie in the Window" are wonderful songs for expanding vocabulary. Let the children come up with the animals names. Substitute new names, make up new verses, and show photos of the animals as you are singing.

5. **CLASSROOM BIG BOOK OF ANIMALS:** Give each child an 11" x 17" piece of paper. Ask them to draw and color a picture of their favorite animal. Then have each child dictate or write a sentence about that animal. When the children have finished, make a cover, punch three holes along the left-hand side, and bind the pages together with yarn. Let each of the children "read" their page to the class. This book will be enjoyed all year long!

6. **CHILDREN'S LITERATURE:** The following books will reinforce animal vocabulary:
   * Brown, Demi. *Touch and Feel Wild Animals.* Dorling Kindersley Publishing. © 1998.
   * Burton, Marilee Robin. *Tails Toes Eyes Ears Nose.* HarperCollins. 1st Edition © 1988.
   * Emberly, Rebecca. *My Animals/Mis animales.* Little, Brown & Company. Bilingual Edition: English & Spanish © 2002.
   * Martin Jr., Bill and Carle, Eric *(illustration)*. *Panda Bear, Panda Bear, What Do You See?* Henry Holt and Company, LLC. © 2003.
   * McCloskey, Robert. *Make Way for Ducklings.* Penguin Group. © Robert McCloskey 1941.
   * Paterson, Betina. *My First Wild Animals.* HarperCollins. © 1991.
   * Wiesner, David. *The Three Pigs.* Clarion Books. © 2001.

3. **IN THE JUNGLE GAME** *(pages 10–11):* Cut out directions and glue to the back of the file folder.

> ***DIRECTIONS:*** Reproduce the gameboard *(pages 10 & 11)*, color and glue on the inside of a file folder. Laminate for durability. Reproduce 4 sets of the wild animal photos *(page 7)* on card stock. Write the words "WILD CARD" on the shark cards. Attach a resealable plastic bag on the back of the file folder for storing the animal cards.
>
> ***HOW TO PLAY:*** Shuffle the cards and lay them face down on the designated square on the gameboard. Use pennies or small objects as markers. Throw a dice or use a numbered spinner to determine how many spaces to move. For example: if the arrow on the spinner stops on the numeral "4," one moves the marker forward four stepping stones. Each time one stops on a stepping stone they get to pick an animal card. If you pick an animal card that you have already collected, you must put it back at the bottom of the deck. If a "wild card" is drawn, the player gets to choose an animal card out of the deck that they do not have already. All players must reach the end of the path. The player with the most animal cards wins! **Watch out** for the "lose a turn" and "extra turn" stones, and the short cuts!

Down On the Farm

Directions: Cut out the animals and paste them in their correct home. Color the picture.

KE-804012 © Key Education
Building Essential Vocabulary

The Pet Store

Directions: Cut out the animals and paste them in their correct location. Color the picture.

In the Jungle

Start

Take an **Extra** turn

Short cut

Place
Animal Cards
Here

Game Board

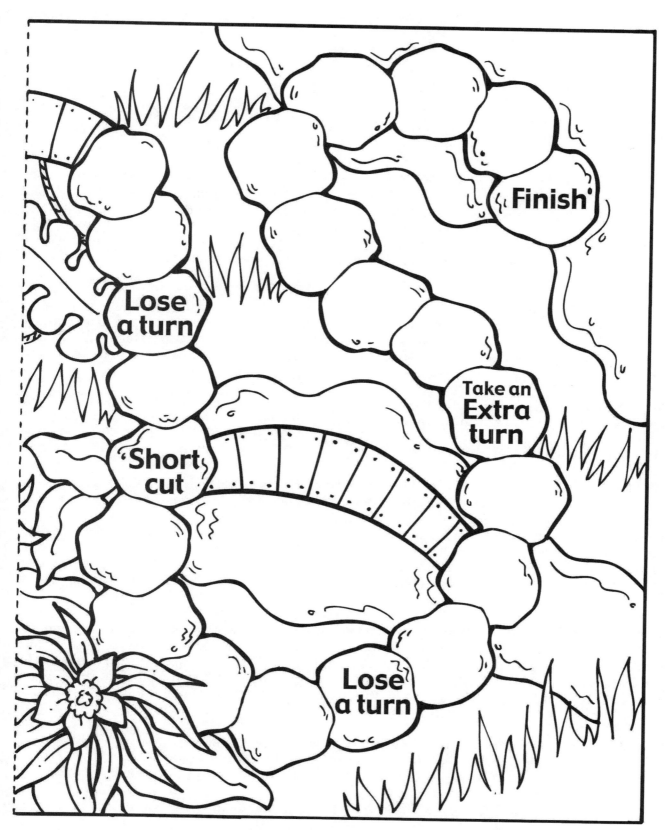

Finish

Lose a turn

Take an Extra turn

Short cut

Lose a turn

(Directions for making and playing "In the Jungle" can be found on page 5.)

 Building Essential Vocabulary

Unit 2: Body Parts

1. **REPRODUCIBLE PHOTO CARDS** are found on pages 13 and 14. *(English and Spanish Vocabulary Lists can be found on page 90.)*

PHOTO CARDS:

1. ankle	7. ear	13. hair	19. neck
2. arm	8. elbow	14. hand	20. nose
3. back	9. eye	15. head	21. shoulder
4. cheek	10. finger	16. knee	22. teeth
5. chest	11. foot	17. leg	23. thumb
6. chin	12. forehead	18. mouth	24. toe

2. **BINGO, LOTTO, AND MEMORY MATCH GAMES** can easily be created with the photo cards. Use the reproducible Lotto game board *(page 88)* and the Bingo game card *(page 89)* to make the games. Complete directions for all three games are found on page 87.

3. **REPRODUCIBLE PAGES: Label a Girl** *(page 15)*, **Label a Boy** *(page 16)*, and **Label a Face** *(page 17)*. Print the name of the specified body part on the proper line. *(You may wish to provide a word bank.)*

   USE FOR ASSESSMENT: For students who are not yet reading or writing, this page can also be used for assessment purposes. To assess receptive skills, say the name of a body part and ask the child to point to that part. To assess expressive skills, point to a body part and ask the child to name it. Record the responses, the date assessed, and place the assessment in the student's file.

4. **SIMON SAYS:** This is a wonderful game for helping children learn the names of their body parts. Practice slowly at first with the children so they understand that the only time they can touch a body part is when they hear the phrase "Simon Says." Increase the speed of the game as the children become more familiar with the vocabulary.

5. **HEAD AND SHOULDERS, KNEES AND TOES:** Here are the lyrics: "Head and shoulders, knees and toes, knees and toes. Head and shoulders, knees and toes, knees and toes. Eyes and ears and mouth and nose. Head and shoulders, knees and toes." Use either a commercially recorded version of this song or you can make your own tape recording. At first, just have the children imitate the actions. Once they have become secure with the actions, encourage them to sing along. Once the children have mastered the words, increase the speed. This song is meant to be sung fast and silly! "The Hokey Pokey" is another great song for learning the names of body parts.

6. **LIFE-SIZE ME:** Let each child take a turn lying down on a piece of butcher paper while another child traces around their body. The children can then color in their own facial features and clothing. As the children are working, walk around and discuss the pictures and extend the vocabulary. For example: "I like the hat you drew on your head." "Are you going to draw tennis shoes on your feet?" "I like the way your elbows are bending." "What color are you going to color your eyes?"

7. **CHILDREN'S LITERATURE:** The following books will reinforce the vocabulary for body parts:
   - Carle, Eric. *From Head to Toe.* Harper Festival. Board Edition © 1999.
   - Hester, Elizabeth. *All About Me (DK Lift-the-Flap Book).* Dorling Kindersley Publishing. 1st Edition © 2003.
   - Katz, Karen. *Where Is Baby's Belly Button?* Little Simon. © 2000.

Photo Cards

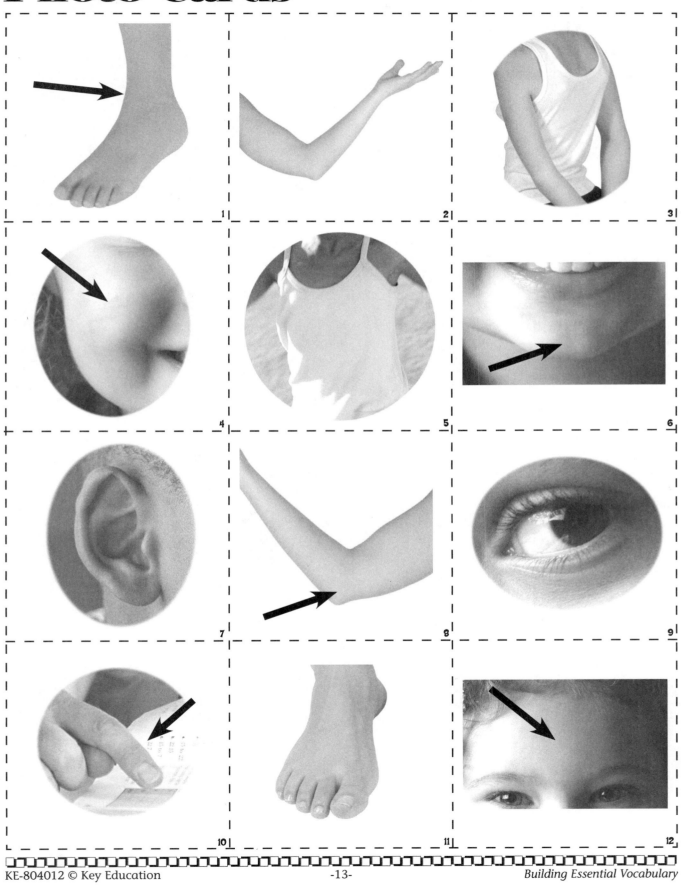

Photo Cards

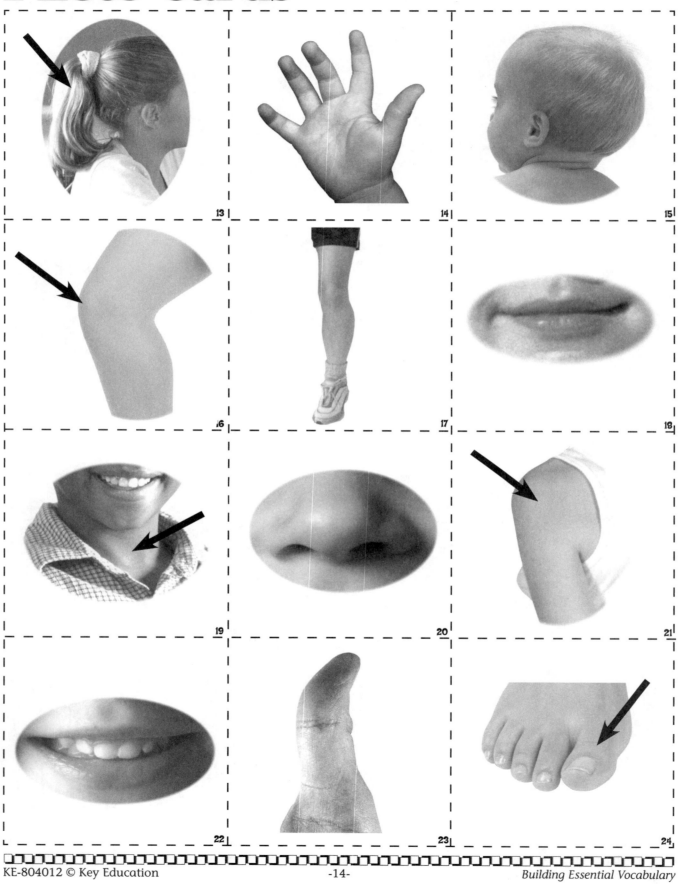

13

14

15

16

17

18

19

20

21

22

23

24

Label a Girl

Directions: See page 12.

Name:_____

Date: _____

Label a Boy

Directions: See page 12.

Name:_____

Date: _____

Label a Face

Directions: See page 12.

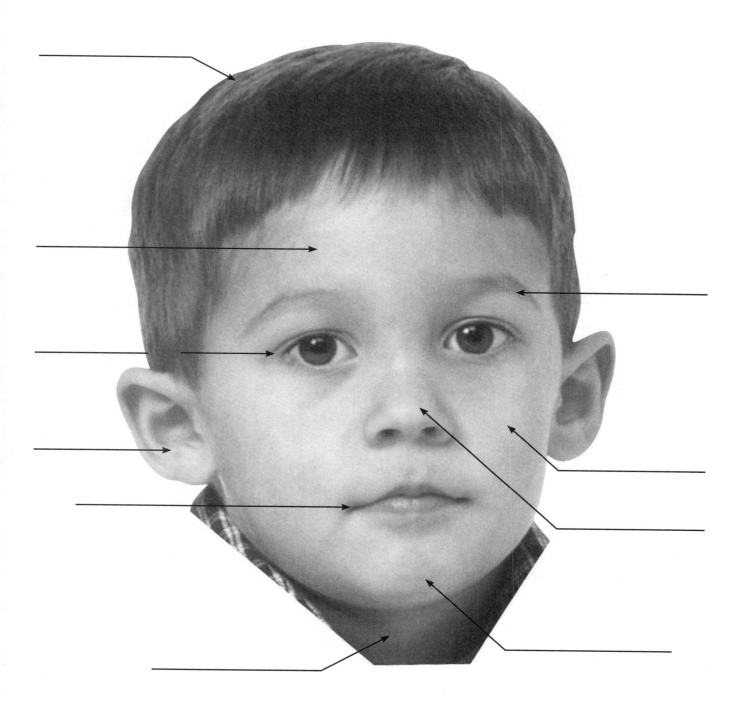

Name: _____ Date: _____

Unit 3: Clothing

1. **REPRODUCIBLE PHOTO CARDS** are found on page 19. *(English and Spanish Vocabulary Lists can be found on page 90.)*

PHOTO CARDS:

1. belt	4. dress	7. pants	10. shirt
2. boots	5. hat	8. purse	11. socks
3. cap	6. jacket	9. shoes	12. underwear

2. **BINGO, LOTTO, AND MEMORY MATCH GAMES** can easily be created with the photo cards. Use the reproducible Lotto game board *(page 88)* and the Bingo game card *(page 89)* to make the games. Complete directions for all three games are found on page 87.

3. **REPRODUCIBLE PAGES:** Complete directions for **Look in the Closet** and **Clothes to Hang Up** can be found on page 21. As the children are working on this activity, model the vocabulary and extend the language experience. For example: "Look, I'm wearing a blue belt. What color is your belt?" "The picture of the shirt has long sleeves. My shirt has short sleeves. And look, the picture of the dress does not have any sleeves." Be sure to point to the item that you are talking about.

4. **DRESS UP EXTRAVAGANZA:** The most effective way to teach children the names of specific clothing items is to name the articles of clothing as the children are playing. Encourage parents to donate clothing *(and shop at garage sales)* that can be placed in a dress-up box. Here is a list of essentials for your dress-up corner: dresses, skirts, blouses, hats, purses, high heels, slacks, shirts, nightgowns, pajamas, robes, slippers, shoes, jackets, boots, belts, jewelry, sport coats, athletic shirts, gowns, aprons, and even wigs.

   PLAY DEPARTMENT STORE: The clothing can also be used for imaginary shopping. Organize the clothes and have the children ask for specific items. Have a cash register, pretend money, and shopping bags handy!

5. **PAPER DOLLS:** Girls especially love playing with paper dolls. Paper dolls can be inexpensively purchased at many large discount stores. Name the clothing as the dolls are dressed.

6. **WEATHER BEAR:** Purchase a commercially published "Weather Bear" bulletin board set or create one of your own. Attach one side of self-stick Velcro™ to the bear and the corresponding piece to an article of clothing. Each morning your students can appropriately dress the bear for the weather. Repeat out loud the names of the clothing being placed on the bear. A large stuffed animal can also be used as a classroom weather mascot. The weather animal can have a special place in the classroom and real children's clothing can be used for dressing it.

7. **CHILDREN'S LITERATURE:** The following books will reinforce the clothing vocabulary:
   - Emberly, Rebecca. *My Clothes/Mi ropa.* Little, Brown & Company. Bilingual Edition: English & Spanish © 2002.
   - Estes, Eleanor. *The Hundred Dresses.* Harcourt. © 2004.
   - Fung, Karen. *Zipper, Buttons and Bows.* Barron's Educational Series, Inc. 1st Edition © 2000.
   - Katz, Karen. *Toes, Ears, and Nose! A Lift-the-Flap Book.* Little Simon. Board Edition © 2003.

Look in the Closet

Clothes to Hang-Up

DIRECTIONS FOR USING
PAGES 20 & 21 AS AN INDEPENDENT ACTIVITY

Reproduce pages 20 and 21 for each child. Have the children color the closet and set it aside. Then have the children cut out all of the photographs of the clothes. Each piece of clothing has a specific place in the closet. Have the children place all the clothing in the closet. The children may glue the clothes in the closet once they are certain they have them in the proper place.

DIRECTIONS FOR USING
PAGES 20 & 21 AS A GAME

PREPARING THE GAME: Reproduce the closet *(page 20)* for each child. This is their individual game board. The children may color their closets before beginning the game.

Then give each child a copy of the clothing found on this page and ask them to cut out all of the photos of the clothes. Walk around the room with a bowl and collect all the clothing photos. *(If the children are too young to cut out such small pieces, the teacher should cut out the clothes ahead of time—making sure that there are twelve individual pieces of clothing for every child.)*

HOW YOU PLAY: The children *(a couple at a time)* come up to the bowl, close their eyes, and take 12 photos of clothes out of the bowl. Once all the children have twelve clothing photos, they go back to their seats and arrange the clothes in the closet. They cannot put two of the same picture in the closet. The duplicate clothing photos must be set aside.

Then have the children walk around and trade clothing squares. For example: "I will trade you my extra belt for the hat I am missing." Everyone wins this game! All of the closets will be full, the children will have socially interacted with each other, and they will have practiced using the vocabulary that they have been learning.

Display the finished closets on a bulletin board!

Unit 4: Colors

1. **REPRODUCIBLE PHOTO CARDS** can be found on page 23. *(English and Spanish Vocabulary Lists can be found on page 90.)*

   PHOTO CARDS:

1.	red	4.	orange	7.	white	10.	pink
2.	blue	5.	purple	8.	brown	11.	grey
3.	yellow	6.	green	9.	black		

2. **BINGO, LOTTO, AND MEMORY MATCH GAMES** can easily be created with the photo cards. Use the reproducible Lotto game board *(page 88)* and the Bingo game card *(page 89)* to make the games. Complete directions for all three games are found on page 87.

3. **PHOTO CARDS:** Each of the reproducible photo cards on page 23 represent a different color. Using a color crayon or marker, draw a line of color around each object to help the students identify the proper colors. Copy four sets of the cards and let the children play "go fish."

4. **COLORFUL PAINT CANS FILE FOLDER GAME:** Reproducible pattern pages and directions can be found on pages 24 and 25.

5. **FIND AND COLOR:** Using a black marker, the teacher should draw one large circle on a piece of white paper. Make as many circles as the number of color words you are reviewing with your students. Tape the circles in different locations around the classroom. One circle at a time, the teacher should choose a color, show the children the color, tell them the name of the color, then walk to the circle and color in only a small portion of that circle. The teacher should continue this until each of the circles has a designated color. The teacher will then call on a student and say the name of a color. That student should then go and pick up that color crayon, walk over to the circle of that color, and color in some more of that circle. Continue the game until the circles are all filled with color.

6. **MUSICAL COLORS:** Cut out construction paper circles in a variety of colors. Have a circle for each student. Lay the colors in a large circle and have the children form a circle around the colors, and then play some music. When the music is playing the children are to walk around the circle. When the music stops—the children should stop and pick up the colored circle that is closest to them.
   Version 1: When the music stops, the children hold up their color and say the name of the color they are holding.
   Version 2: When the music stops, the children hold up their colors and then group themselves together with the children who are holding the same color circles.

7. **CHILDREN'S LITERATURE:** The following books will reinforce color word vocabulary:
   - Carle, Eric. *Grouchy Ladybug.* HarperCollins Children's Books. © 1977.
   - Cote, Pamela. *What Color Is It?/¿Qué color es éste?.* Houghton Mifflin Company. © 2002.
   - Ehlert, Lois. *Planting a Rainbow.* Harcourt. © 1992.
   - Emberley, Rebecca. *My Colors/Mis colores.* Little, Brown & Company. © 2000.
   - Graves, Kimberlee. *Colors of My Day.* Rebound by Sagebrush. © 1997.
   - Hoban, Tana. *Of Colors and Things.* HarperTrophy. 1st Mulberry Edition © 1996.
   - Lionni, Leo. *Color of His Own.* Bantam Doubleday Dell Books for Young Readers. © 1997.
   - Martin, Bill Jr. and Carle, Eric. *Brown Bear, Brown Bear, What Do You See?* Henry Holt and Company, Inc. © 1996.
   - Walsh, Ellen Stoll. *Mouse Paint.* Red Wagon Books. Board Edition © 1995.

Photo Cards

Using a color crayon, draw a line of color around each object to help students learn to identify the colors.

Colorful Paint Cans

File Folder Game

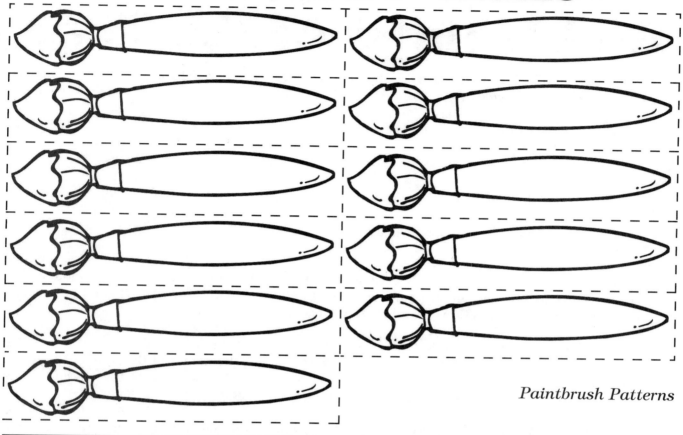

Paintbrush Patterns

HOW TO MAKE "THE COLORFUL PAINT CANS FILE FOLDER GAME"

Paint Cans: Copy page 24 and color each paint can a different color. Tape or glue the colored paint can page onto the left inside half of a file folder. Laminate for durability. Attach a small resealable plastic bag on the inside right half of the file folder that can be used for storing the paintbrushes and directions.

Paintbrushes: Copy page 25, color each paintbrush to match the colors of the paint cans, and cut them out along the dotted lines. Laminate for durability. Attach a small piece of self-stick Velcro™ on the top oval of each paint can. Place the corresponding piece of Velcro™ onto the back of each paintbrush tip. The children can sit, name the colors, and stick each paintbrush onto its matching paint can.

Extra Note: The teacher should choose whether or not she wishes to include color words in this game. Younger children may simply use the game with the colors. Older children may play the game by also using color words.

HOW TO PLAY "THE COLORFUL PAINT CAN FILE FOLDER GAME" AS A GROUP

Group Play: All players will need their own file folder game and eleven paintbrushes. The teacher will also need to have prepared a color spinner. Using a paper plate, divide the plate into eleven sections *(like a pie),* and color the sections the same colors as the paint cans. Cut a plastic arrow from the lid of a margarine container and attach to the plate with a brad. The children then take turns spinning the arrow. When the arrow stops on a color, the child whose turn it is puts that color paintbrush on the paint can. If a paintbrush is already on the paint can, they lose their turn and hand the spinner to the next player. The first child to put all the paintbrushes on the paint cans is the winner!

Unit 5: Days of the Week and Months of the Year

1. **REPRODUCIBLE PHOTO CARDS** are found on pages 27–28. *(English and Spanish Vocabulary Lists can be found on page 91.)*

(page 27)   **PHOTO CARDS:**   *(page 28)*

1. Sunday	1. January	7. July
2. Monday	2. February	8. August
3. Tuesday	3. March	9. September
4. Wednesday	4. April	10. October
5. Thursday	5. May	11. November
6. Friday	6. June	12. December
7. Saturday		

2. **BINGO, LOTTO, AND MEMORY MATCH GAMES** can easily be created with the photo cards. Use the reproducible Lotto game board *(page 88)* and the Bingo game card *(page 89)* to make the games. Complete directions for all three games are found on page 87.

3. **THE MULBERRY BUSH:** Learning the days of the week is a difficult task for some children. The song, "The Mulberry Bush" can help children to remember the names of the days of the week. Reproduce a set of the days of the week photo cards *(page 27)* for each of the students. The children can place the photo cards in the correct sequence as they sing the song.

   DAYS OF THE WEEK BIG BOOK: "The Mulberry Bush" will also make a wonderful big book. Divide the children into seven groups. Provide each group with a large piece of poster board, crayons and markers. Then have each group illustrate one verse of the song. To finish, make a cover and bind the pages together.

4. **MONTHS OF THE YEAR PHOTO CARD ACTIVITIES:** Each of the months of the year photo cards represents something that happens during that month. January is a cold and snowy month; February has Valentine's Day; March has St. Patrick's Day; April showers . . . bring May flowers; many children play baseball during the month of June; 4th of July fireworks; August is the hottest month of the year; many schools begin in September; Halloween happens in October; leaves change color in November; and there are many different holidays in December. Talk to the children about how the seasons change. Look at books that show photographs of how the seasons change.

5. **CALENDAR ACTIVITIES:** A blank reproducible calendar can be found on page 29. Every month give each child a blank calendar. Have the children add the days of the week, record the weather, and write down any special activities that take place during the month on their calendars.

6. **CHILDREN'S LITERATURE:** The following books will reinforce the days of the week and months of the year vocabulary:
   - Carle, Eric. *Today is Monday.* Putnam Publishing Group. Reprint Edition © 1997.
   - Gibbons, Gail. *The Reasons for Seasons.* Holiday House. Reprint Edition © 1996.
   - Sendak, Maurice. *Chicken Soup with Rice: A Book of Months.* HarperCollins Children's Books. Reprint Edition © 1990.
   - Ward, Cindy and de Paola, Tomie. *Cookie's Week.* Putnam Juvenile. © 1997.

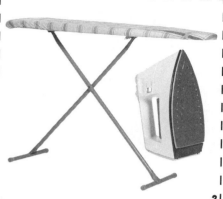

The Mulberry Bush

Chorus
Here we go 'round the mulberry bush.
The mulberry bush,
The mulberry bush.
Here we go 'round the mulberry bush,
So early in the morning.

Verse 1
This is the way we go to church.
Go to church, go to church.
This is the way we go to church.
So early SUNDAY morning.

Verse 2
This is the way we wash our clothes.
Wash our clothes, wash our clothes.
This is the way we wash our clothes.
So early MONDAY morning.

Verse 3
This is the way we iron our clothes.
Iron our clothes, iron our clothes.
This is the way we iron our clothes.
So early TUESDAY morning.

Verse 4
This is the way we mend our clothes.
Mend our clothes, mend our clothes.
This is the way we mend our clothes.
So early WEDNESDAY morning.

Verse 5
This is the way we sweep the floor.
Sweep the floor, sweep the floor.
This is the way we sweep the floor.
So early THURSDAY morning.

Verse 6
This is the way we scrub the floor.
Scrub the floor, scrub the floor.
This is the way we scrub the floor.
So early FRIDAY morning.

Verse 7
This is the way we bake our bread.
Bake our bread, bake our bread.
This is the way we bake our bread.
So early SATURDAY morning.

MAKE UP YOUR VERSES

Encourage the children
to make up their own verses.
Choose activities that the
children do during the week. *For
example:* This is the way we...
bounce the ball;
print our names;
eat our lunch;
wash our hands; or
play with our friends.

Calendar

Unit 6: Emotions

1. **REPRODUCIBLE PHOTO CARDS** are found on page 31. (*English and Spanish Vocabulary Lists can be found on page 91.*)

   PHOTO CARDS:

1. angry	4. grouchy	7. scared	10. silly
2. bored	5. happy	8. serious	11. surprised
3. excited	6. sad	9. shy	12. tired

2. **BINGO, LOTTO, AND MEMORY MATCH GAMES** can easily be created with the photo cards. Use the reproducible Lotto game board (*page 88*) and the Bingo game card (*page 89*) to make the games. Complete directions for all three games are found on page 87.

3. **HOW DO YOU FEEL?:** Before beginning this activity, show the children the photo cards and talk about the different emotions. Then give each child a copy of page 32. Using a mirror, have the children practice making a variety of faces; happy, sad, surprised, angry, tired, etc. Give the children pencils and let them experiment with drawing all sorts of different emotions on the face outlines.

4. **NOISY EMOTIONS:** Emotions are not only shown by facial expressions, but you can also hear emotion and know the way that people are feeling by the sounds they make. What sounds would people make if they were sad? Happy? Mad? Excited? Children think this is a very silly activity. There will be lots of giggles!

5. **FINISH THE SENTENCE:** Begin a sentence and have the children fill in the blank. Here are some examples: _____ makes me happy. _____ makes me sad. _____ makes me angry. When the children are able to respond to this simple sentence structure you can make it more difficult by using a variety of sentences, such as: I was happy when _____. I was sad when _____. One thing that makes me angry is _____.

6. **IF YOU'RE HAPPY AND YOU KNOW IT:** Sing the song, "If You're Happy and You Know It." Make up new verses and actions, such as, "If you're mad and you know it, stamp your feet; If you're tired and you know it take a nap."

7. **CHILDREN'S LITERATURE:** The following books will reinforce the vocabulary that describes emotion:
   - Bang, Molly. *When Sophie Gets Angry—Really, Really Angry... .* (Caldecott Honor Book). Scholastic. © 1999.
   - Boynton, Sandra. *A is for Angry.* Workman Publishing. © 1987.
   - Cain, Janan. *The Way I Feel.* Parenting Press. © 2000.
   - Crary, Elizabeth, et al. *When You're Happy: And You Know It (Feelings for Little Children Series).* Parenting Press. © 1996.
   - Crary, Elizabeth, et al. *When You're Mad: And You Know It (Feelings for Little Children Series).* Parenting Press. © 1996.
   - Curtis, Jamie Lee and Cornell, Laura. *It's Hard to Be Five: Learning How to Work My Control Panels.* Joanna Colter. © 2004.
   - Curtis, Jamie Lee and Cornell, Laura. *Today I Feel Silly: And Other Moods That Make My Day.* Joanna Colter. 1st Edition © 1998.
   - Emberly, Rebecca. *How Do I Feel?/¿Cómo me siento?* Houghton Mifflin. Bilingual Board Edition: English & Spanish © 2002.
   - Litchenheld, Tom. *What Are You So Grumpy About?* Little, Brown & Company. 1st Edition © 2003.

How Do You Feel?

Directions: See page 30.

Name: _____ Date: _____

Unit 7: Family/People

1. **REPRODUCIBLE PHOTO CARDS** are found on page 34. (*English and Spanish Vocabulary Lists can be found on page 91.*)

PHOTO CARDS:

1. baby
2. sister
   daughter
   granddaughter
3. brother
   son
   grandson
4. mother and daughter
5. father and son
6. grandmother
   grandfather
7. man
8. woman
9. family
10. boy
11. girl
12. friends

2. **BINGO, LOTTO, AND MEMORY MATCH GAMES** can easily be created with the photo cards. Use the reproducible Lotto game board (*page 88*) and the Bingo game card (*page 89*) to make the games. Complete directions for all three games are found on page 87.

3. **LABEL THE FAMILY:** This reproducible activity is found on page 35. Print the name of each family member on the appropriate line. (*The teacher may wish to provide a word bank.*)

   USE FOR ASSESSMENT: For students who are not yet reading or writing, this page can also be used for assessment purposes. To assess receptive skills, say the name of the family member and ask the child to point to that person. To assess expressive skills, point to a family member and ask the child to name the person. Record the responses, the date assessed, and place the assessment in the student's file.

4. **MY FAMILY TREE:** This reproducible activity is found on page 36. Ask the parents to send some family photos to school. Be sure to tell the parents that the photos will be returned to them unharmed. Make black and white photocopies of the original photos. The children can then cut out the faces of some of their own family members and glue them onto their family tree. When completed, ask the children to show their classmates their family tree and say the names of the people on their tree.

5. **CHILDREN'S LITERATURE:** The following books will reinforce the vocabulary for family members and people:
   - Aliki. *We Are Best Friends.* HarperTrophy. Reprint Edition © 1987.
   - Berhard, Emery. *A Ride on Mother's Back: A Day of Carrying Baby Around the World.* Gulliver Books. 1st Edition © 1996.
   - Flournoy, Valerie. *The Patchwork Quilt.* Dial Books. 1st Edition © 1985.
   - Johnson, Angela and Soman, David. *Daddy Calls Me Man.* Orchard Books. © 2000.
   - Johnson, Angela and Soman, David. *Tell Me a Story, Mama.* Orchard Books. 1st Edition © 1989.
   - Johnson, Angela and Soman, David. *When I Am Old With You.* Franklin Watts, Inc. Reprint Edition © 1993.
   - Lenski, Lois. *The Little Family.* Random House Books for Young Readers. 1st Random Edition. © 2002.
   - Levinson, Riki. *I Go with My Family to Grandma's.* Puffin Books. Reprint Edition © 1986.
   - Long, Earlene. *Gone Fishing.* Houghton Mifflin. © 1984.
   - Parr, Todd. *The Family Book.* Megan Tingley. 1st Edition © 2003.
   - Rotner, Shelley and Kelly, Sheila. *Lots of Moms.* Dial. 1st Edition © 1996.
   - Rylant, Cynthia. *The Relatives Came.* Alladin. Reprint Edition © 1993.
   - Wallner, Alexandra. *Farmer in the Dell.* Holiday House. 1st Edition © 1998.

Label the Family

Directions: See page 33.

Name: _____ Date: _____

My Family Tree

Directions: See page 33.

Name: _____ Date: _____

Building Essential Vocabulary

Unit 8: Furniture

1. **REPRODUCIBLE PHOTO CARDS** are found on page 38. *(English and Spanish Vocabulary Lists can be found on page 91.)*

PHOTO CARDS:

1. bed	4. clock	7. mirror	10. table
2. bookshelves	5. desk	8. sofa	11. telephone
3. chair	6. lamp	9. stool	12. television

2. **BINGO, LOTTO, AND MEMORY MATCH GAMES** can easily be created with the photo cards. Use the reproducible Lotto game board *(page 88)* and the Bingo game card *(page 89)* to make the games. Complete directions for all three games are found on page 87.

3. **FURNISH THE HOUSE:** Copy page 39 for each child. Have the children color the house and then cut the furniture photos out along the dotted lines. Have the children place the furniture in any arrangement they want. Once the children have decided where they like their furniture, they can use glue sticks to glue the furniture in place.

4. **DOLL HOUSES AND BUILDING BLOCKS:** Playing with a doll house is an effective way to teach vocabulary because it provides children with concrete examples. Play with the children and model the vocabulary. For example: "Let's put the baby to bed. The boy can sit on the chair." If the boys are reluctant to play with the doll house, provide them with the experience of building furniture using blocks. Beds, chairs, sofas, tables, and many other pieces of furniture are easily constructed with blocks and a little imagination.

   HOLD A FURNITURE BUILDING CONTEST: Have the children work in teams. The teacher says the name of a piece of furniture and the children must work together to construct it.

5. **PLAY HIDE AND SEEK:** The teacher is "it" and closes her eyes while the children hide. Each time the teacher finds a child they must say where they were hiding: by the chair; under the table; etc. This will build their vocabulary and increase their understanding of positional concepts.

6. **PHOTO CARD FURNITURE, GAME ONE:** Reproduce the furniture photo cards *(page 38)* for each of the children. Have the children lay the cards face-up in front of them. The teacher says the name of a piece of furniture and the children pick up the photo as fast as they can. Children love this game and it can be used with any of the themes presented in this book.

7. **PHOTO CARD FURNITURE, GAME TWO:** Reproduce one set of the furniture photo cards *(page 38)*. Have the children sit in a circle. Place all twelve cards face-up in the middle of the circle so that everyone can see them. Have the children close their eyes and then remove or turn over one card. The first child to guess which card is gone receives a point. Increase the difficulty of the game by increasing the number of cards removed or turned over.

8. **CHILDREN'S LITERATURE:** The following books will reinforce furniture vocabulary:
   - Arnold, Tedd. *No Jumping on the Bed.* Dial Books for Young Readers. 1st Edition © 1987.
   - Buchanan, Heather S. *George and Matilda Mouse and the Doll's House.* Simon & Schuster. © 1988.
   - Emberly, Rebecca. *My House/Mi casa.* Little, Brown & Company. Bilingual Edition: English & Spanish © 1993.
   - Hirashima, Jean *(illustrator)* and Henry, Allison *(illustrator)*. *Hello Kitty's House and Garden.* Henry N. Abrams, Inc. Board Edition © 2003.
   - LeSieg, Theo. *In a People House.* Random House Books for Young Readers. © 1972
   - Williams, Vera B. *A Chair for My Mother.* HarperTrophy. Reprint Edition © 1984.

Photo Cards

1
2
3
4
5
6
7
8
9
10
11
12

Furnish the House

Directions:
See page 37.

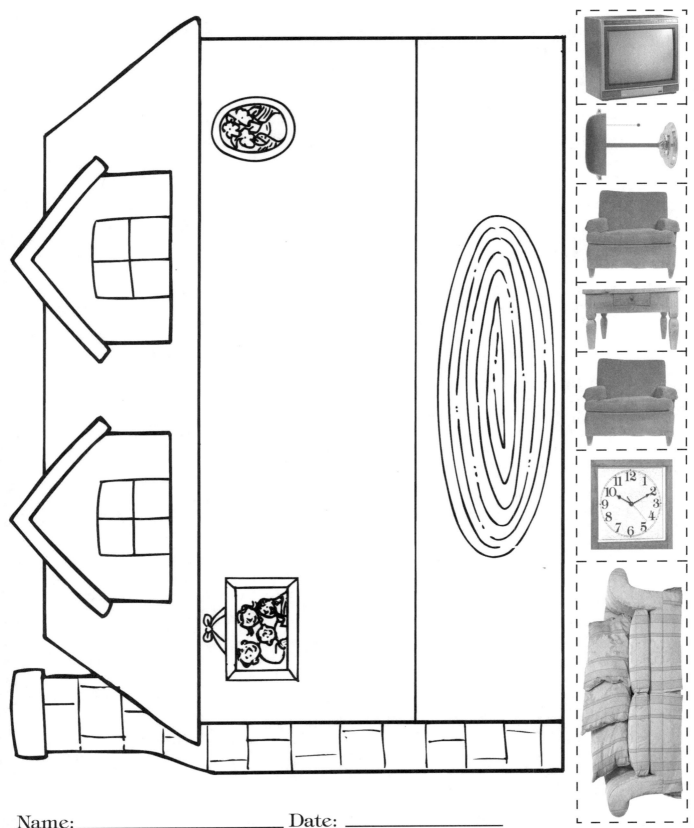

Name: _____ Date: _____

Unit 9: Everyday Objects

1. **REPRODUCIBLE PHOTO CARDS** are found on pages 41–43. *(English and Spanish Vocabulary Lists can be found on page 91–92.)*

PHOTO CARDS:

(Bathroom Objects)
1. bathtub
2. comb
3. cup
4. hairdryer
5. sink
6. mirror
7. soap
8. toilet
9. toilet paper
10. toothbrushes
11. toothpaste
12. towels

(Household Objects)
13. books
14. camera
15. car
16. computer
17. eye glasses
18. fan
19. flowers
20. house
21. keys
22. pillow
23. vacuum
24. window

(Kitchen Objects)
25. broom
26. dishes
27. fork
28. iron
29. knife
30. pan
31. plate
32. refrigerator
33. coffee cup
34. spoon
35. stove
36. toaster

2. **BINGO, LOTTO, AND MEMORY MATCH GAMES** can easily be created with the photo cards. Use the reproducible Lotto game board *(page 88)* and the Bingo game card *(page 89)* to make the games. Complete directions for all three games are found on page 87.

3. **I SPY BATHROOM THINGS:** Reproducible activity and directions are found on page 44.

4. **I SPY KITCHEN THINGS:** Reproducible activity and directions are found on page 45.

5. **PICTIONARY:** Copy the photo cards found on pages 41–43 and place them in a container. Have a child come up and pick a photo card out of the container. Have the child draw the picture with chalk on the blackboard or with a marker on chart paper. The first child to correctly guess the name of the object being drawn gets to be the next child to pick a card.

6. **ROOM TAG:** Play a game of tag. When tagged, the child must say the name of an object that is found in that room. For example, during kitchen tag, the children might say either spoon, pan, stove, or dish.

7. **CUT AND PASTE FUN:** Tape two large pieces of paper on a wall or blackboard. Tape some toilet paper on the first piece of paper and tape a plastic spoon on the second piece of paper. Have the children look through newspapers, magazines, and catalogs for pictures of objects that belong in either the bathroom or the kitchen. Cut out those objects and tape or paste them on the correct piece of paper.

8. **CHILDREN'S LITERATURE:** The following books will reinforce the vocabulary for everyday objects:
   - Amery, Heather and Cartwright, Stephen. *The Usborne First Thousand Words (Picture Words Book)*. Usborne Books. Revised Edition © 2003.
   - Arnold, Tedd. *No More Water in the Tub!* Puffin Books. Reprint Edition © 1998.
   - Conrad, Pam. *The Tub People*. HarperTrophy. 1st Harper Edition © 1995.
   - Crowther, Robert. *Robert Crowther's Amazing Pop-Up House of Inventions & Hundreds of Fabulous Facts About Where You Live*. Candlewick Press. Pop-Up Edition © 2000.
   - Gorner, Terri. *1001 Things to Spot in the Town*. E.D.C. Publishing. © 2001.
   - Litchfield, Jo, et all. *The Usborne Book of Everyday Words*. E.D.C. Publishing. © 1999.
   - Rex, Michael. *Pie is Cherry (Kitchen Things)*. Henry Holt & Company. © 2001.

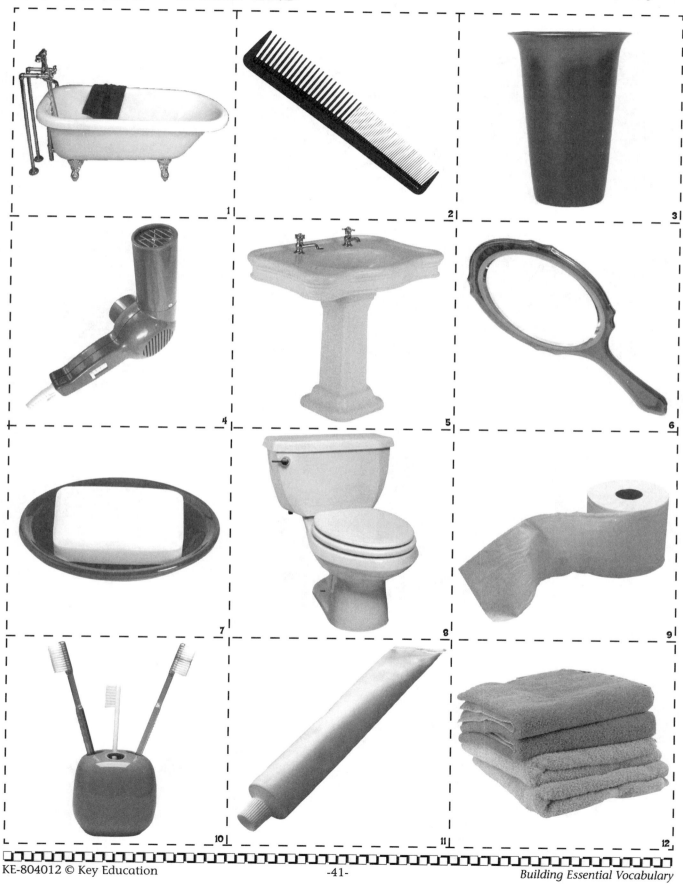

Photo Cards

13

14

15

16

17

18

19

20

21

22

23

24

I Spy Bathroom Things

Name: _____ Date: _____

Directions: Copy this page for each child. Explain to the children that they are going to play "I Spy."
Version 1: The teacher says the name of an object and the children color that object.
Version 2: (Difficult) The teacher describes an object and the children color that object.
Assessment: This page can also be used for documenting vocabulary development. The teacher points to the objects and the child names the objects— or the teacher names the objects and the child points to them.

I Spy Kitchen Things

Name: _____ Date: _____

Directions: Copy this page for each child. Explain to the children that they are going to play "I Spy."
Version 1: The teacher says the name of an object and the children color that object.
Version 2: (Difficult) The teacher describes an object and the children color that object.
Assessment: This page can also be used for documenting vocabulary development. The teacher points to the objects and the child names the objects— or the teacher names the objects and the child points to them.

Unit 10: Food

1. **REPRODUCIBLE PHOTO CARDS** are found on pages 47–50. *(English and Spanish Vocabulary Lists can be found on page 92.)*

PHOTO CARDS:

(page 47)

1. apple
2. asparagus
3. bananas
4. bread
5. broccoli
6. butter
7. cake
8. carrots
9. cauliflower
10. celery
11. cereal
12. cheese

(page 48)

13. chicken
14. coffee
15. cookies
16. corn
17. doughnut
18. eggs
19. fish
20. french fries
21. grapes
22. grapefruit
23. green beans
24. hamburger

(page 49)

25. hot dog
26. ice cream
27. lemon
28. milk
29. muffin
30. mushrooms
31. orange juice
32. oranges
33. pancakes
34. pears
35. pie
36. pineapple

(page 50)

37. popcorn
38. potato
39. pretzel
40. salad
41. sandwich
42. spagetti
43. strawberries
44. taco
45. tomato
46. waffel
47. water
48. watermelon

2. **BINGO, LOTTO, AND MEMORY MATCH GAMES** can easily be created with the photo cards. Use the reproducible Lotto game board *(page 88)* and the Bingo game card *(page 89)* to make the games. Complete directions for all three games are found on page 87.

3. **STOCK THE GROCERY STORE:** Reproducible activity and directions are found on pages 51 and 52.

4. **FOOD TASTING EXPERIENCES:** Plan a variety of food tasting experiences. Organize this activity by the types of food being tasted: fruits, vegetables, dairy products, breads, and meat & protein. To begin the experience, show the children the whole food, such as an apple. Say the word several times and describe it: "It is round and red." Cut the apple into "taste-size" pieces and share them with the children. Extend the language experience by describing the taste: "The apple is sweet." It is also fun to make the tasting experience a guessing game.

5. **MAKE YOUR OWN PIZZA:** Give each child a paper plate, construction paper, markers, scissors, glue, and magazines. Ask the children to create their favorite pizza. As an example, the teacher should make a paper plate pizza ahead of time and describe her pizza to the children: "I love pineapple, olives, cheese, tomatoes, and chicken on my pizza."

6. **CHILDREN'S LITERATURE:** The following books will reinforce the food vocabulary:
   - Buono, Anthony and Nemerson, Roy. *The Race Against Junk Food.* HCom. 1st Edition © 1997.
   - Ehlert, Lois. *Eating the Alphabet: Fruits and Vegetables from A to Z.* Harcourt Children's Books. 1st Edition © 1989.
   - Ehlert, Lois. *Growing Vegetable Soup.* Voyager Books. Reprint Edition © 1990.
   - Emberly, Rebecca. *My Foods/Mi comida.* Little, Brown & Company. Bilingual Edition: English & Spanish © 2002.
   - Fleming, Denise. *Lunch.* Henry Holt and Company. Board Edition © 1998.
   - Leedy, Loreen. *The Edible Pyramid.* Holiday House. Reprint Edition © 1996.
   - Sears, Martha and Sears, William and Kelly, Christie Watts. *Eat Healthy, Feel Great.* Little, Brown. 1st Edition © 2002.
   - Sharmat, Mitchell. *Gregory, the Terrible Eater.* Scholastic. Reissue Edition © 1985.

Food

-48-

Building Essential Vocabulary

25

26

27

28

29

30

31

32

33

34

35

36

Photo Cards

37

38

39

40

41

42

43

44

45

46

47

48

Stock the Grocery Store

Name: _____

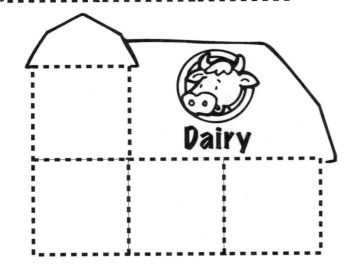

Food to Stock the Grocery Store

STOCK THE GROCERY STORE

Copy pages 51 and 52 for each child. Have the children cut out the food photos along the dotted lines. Review all of the food names with the children. Tell the children that the grocery store is empty and that they must fill up the store before people come to shop.

EXTRA FUN ACTIVITY — PLAN YOUR OWN MEALS

Reproduce the food photo cards *(pages 47–50)* for each child. Provide the children with paper plates, scissors, crayons, and glue. The goal is for the children to create three meals: breakfast, lunch, and dinner. The children should sort the food photo cards according to the different meals. They should then plan one meal at a time by placing the food photo cards on a plate. The children can glue the food to the plate once they have finalized their decisions.

SIGN-LANGUAGE FOOD ACTIVITY

In addition to learning "food vocabulary," it is also fun to teach the children some of the American Sign-Language "signs" for food.

Unit 11: Numbers

1. **REPRODUCIBLE PHOTO CARD PUZZLES** are found on pages 54–57. Copy the number puzzles, cut out along the dotted lines, laminate for durability, and enjoy matching the numeral to the correct set of photo objects. *(English and Spanish Vocabulary Lists can be found on pages 92–93.)*

PHOTO CARDS:

1 – one	6 – six	11 – eleven	16 – sixteen
2 – two	7 – seven	12 – twelve	17 – seventeen
3 – three	8 – eight	13 – thirteen	18 – eighteen
4 – four	9 – nine	14 – fourteen	19 – nineteen
5 – five	10 – ten	15 – fifteen	20 – twenty

2. **BINGO, LOTTO, AND MEMORY MATCH GAMES** can easily be created with the photo cards. Use the reproducible Lotto game board *(page 88)* and the Bingo game card *(page 89)* to make the games. Complete directions for all three games are found on page 87.

3. **FLASH CARD TOSS:** You will need a box of number flash cards, a bean bag, and either a vinyl tablecloth or window shade to be used as a game mat. Use a black magic marker and print numbers on the plastic game mat. Have the children sit around the mat. Then have one child at a time draw a number flash card, say the name of the number, and then attempt to toss the bean bag onto that same number on the mat.

4. **MAKE A NUMBER SET:** Play some music while the children walk around the classroom. The teacher calls out a number and the children must scramble and get together in a group that equals the number called.

5. **TEXTURE NUMBERS:** Using heavy cardboard, make a large set of number flash cards. Trace over each number with white glue and then sprinkle sand on the glue. When the glue is dry, the children can trace the number with their fingers and "feel" and say the number. Make the flash cards large enough so that a number of buttons, equaling the number on the card, can also be glued onto the card.

6. **CHILDREN'S LITERATURE:** The following books will reinforce the vocabulary of numbers:
   - Christelow, Eileen. *Five Little Monkeys Jumping on the Bed.* Clarion Books. Board Edition © 1998.
   - Crews, Donald. *Ten Black Dots.* HarperTrophy. Revised Edition © 1995.
   - Ernst, Lisa Campbell. *Up to Ten and Down Again.* Lothrop, Lee & Shephard Books. © 1986.
   - Hamm, Diane Johnston. *How Many Feet in Bed?* Aladdin. © 1991.
   - Hoban, Tana. *Count and See.* Simon & Schuster Children's Publishing. © 1972.
   - Hutchins, Pat. *1 Hunter.* HarperTrophy. © 1982.
   - Mitsumasa, Anno. *Anno's Counting Book.* HarperTrophy. © 1976.
   - Sloat, Terri. *From One to One Hundred.* Puffin Books. © 1991.
   - Walsh, Ellen Stoll. *Mouse Counts.* Red Wagon Books. Board Edition © 1995.

Number Puzzles

1

2

3

4

5

Number Puzzles

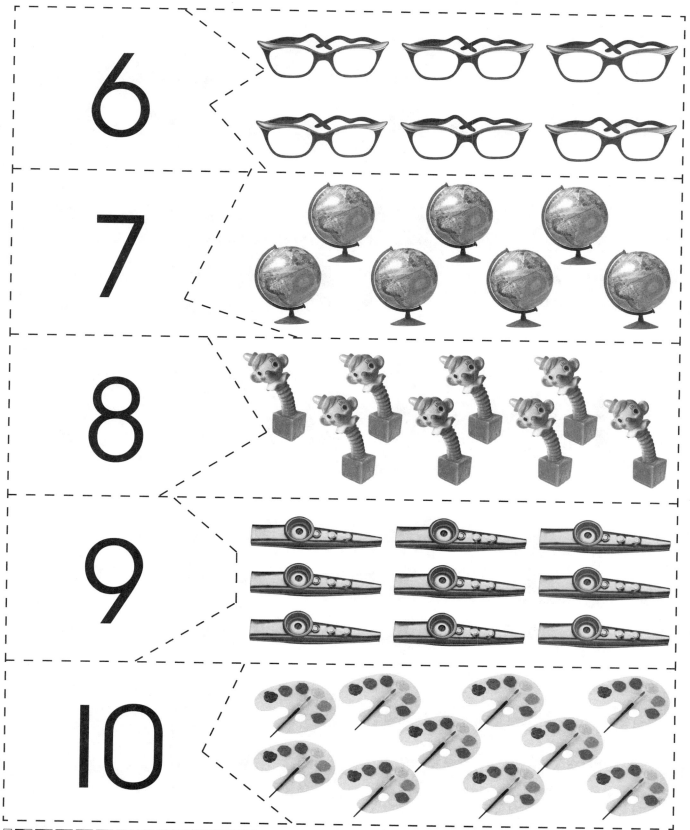

6

7

8

9

10

Number Puzzles

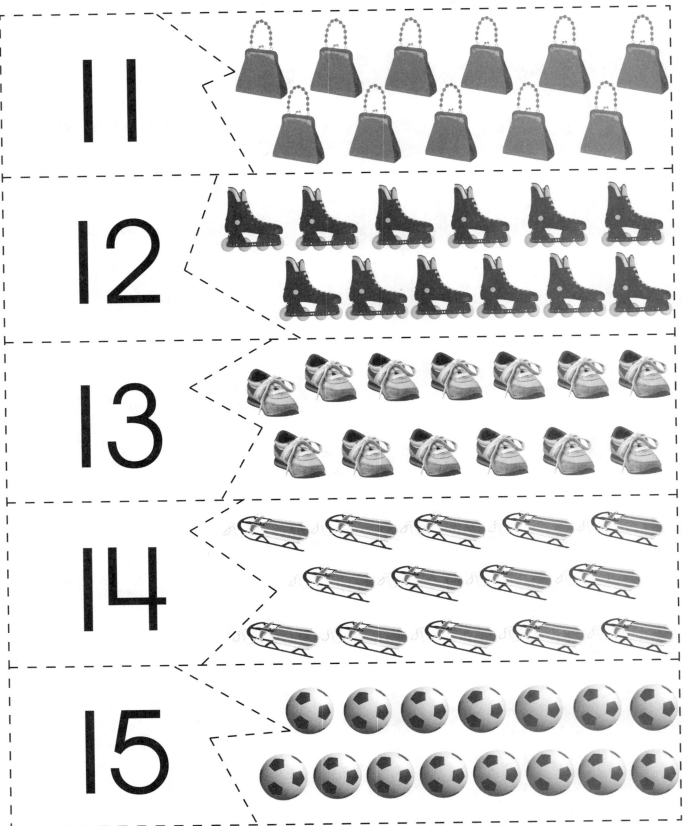

11

12

13

14

15

Number Puzzles

16

17

18

19

20

Unit 12: Opposites

1. **REPRODUCIBLE PHOTO CARDS** are found on pages 59–62. *(English and Spanish Vocabulary Lists can be found on page 93.)*

PHOTO CARDS:

(page 59)

1. front	7. big
2. back	8. little
3. young	9. cold
4. old	10. hot
5. awake	11. happy
6. asleep	12. sad

(page 60)

13. in	19. winter
14. out	20. summer
15. clean	21. few
16. dirty	22. many
17. man	23. fast
18. woman	24. slow

(page 61)

25. girl	31. tall
26. boy	32. short
27. wet	33. night
28. dry	34. day
29. near	35. full
30. far	36. empty

(page 62)

37. closed	43. hard
38. open	44. soft
39. loud	45. old
40. quiet	46. new
41. on	47. white
42. off	48. black

2. **BINGO, LOTTO, AND MEMORY MATCH GAMES** can easily be created with the photo cards. Use the reproducible Lotto game board *(page 88)* and the Bingo game card *(page 89)* to make the games. Complete directions for all three games are found on page 87.

3. **PANTOMIMING OPPOSITE PAIRS:** Have the children work in pairs. Give each pair of children a set of opposite cards—for example, one pair of students would be given the cards for "young" and "old." The children each pantomime one of the cards while the rest of the children in the class guess what they are doing. For example: the child who has the "young" card might pantomime crying or crawling like a baby and the other child with the "old" card might walk hunched over and pretend he is holding a cane.

4. **MAKE AN OPPOSITES BIG BOOK:** Read a variety of the opposite books listed below. Once the children have an understanding of what opposites are, let them design their own book. Before they begin working on their book, give each child an opposite card. Have the children walk around the room to discover who has their matching opposite. Once the children have found each other, have them create a page together for the classroom big book.

5. **CHILDREN'S LITERATURE:** The following books will reinforce the vocabulary of opposites:
   - Bridwell, Norman. *Clifford's Opposites.* Scholastic, Inc. © 2000.
   - Burningham, John. *Opposites.* Candlewick Press. © 2003.
   - Falconer, Ian. *Olivia's Opposites.* Simon & Schuster Children's Books. © 2002.
   - Fox, Mem. *Where Is the Green Sheep?* Harcourt. © 2004.
   - Hoban, Tana. *Exactly the Opposites.* William Morrow & Company, Inc. © 1997.
   - Huelin, Jodi. *Harold and the Purple Crayon: Opposites.* HarperCollins Children's Books. © 2004.
   - Patricelli, Leslie. *Yummy Yucky.* Candlewick Press. © 2003.
   - Seuss, Dr. *One Fish, Two Fish, Red Fish, Blue Fish.* Random House, Inc. © 1976.
   - Seuss, Dr. *The Foot Book: Dr. Seuss's Wacky Book of Opposites.* Random House, Inc. © 1996.

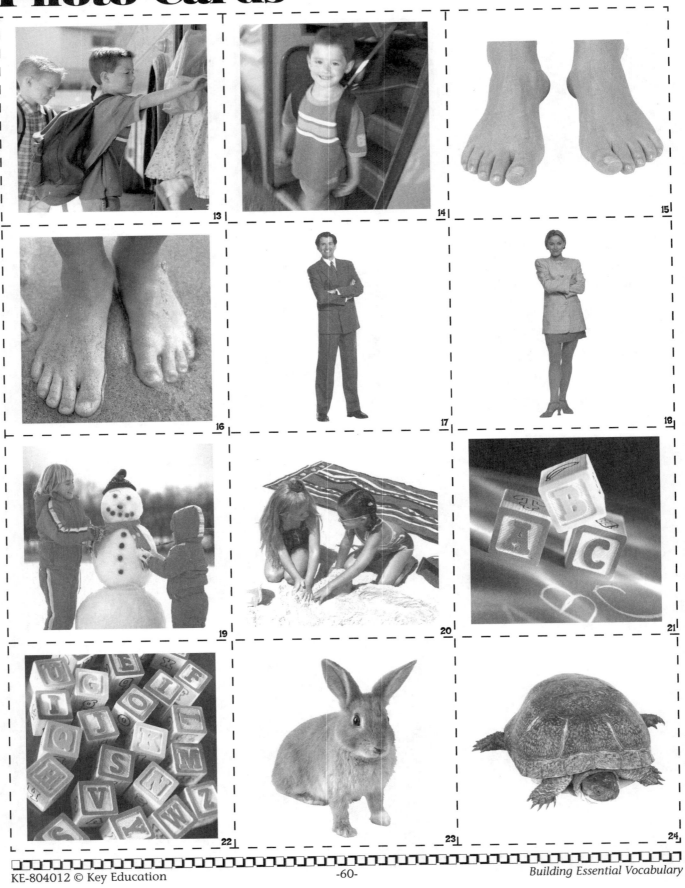

Photo Cards

25

26

27

28

29

30

31

32

33

34

35

36

Unit 13: People in the Neighborhood

1. **REPRODUCIBLE PHOTO CARDS** are found on pages 64–65. *(English and Spanish Vocabulary Lists can be found on pages 93–94.)*

PHOTO CARDS:

1. baker	7. doctor	13. librarian	19. seamstress
2. business people	8. delivery person	14. mail carrier	20. teacher
3. construction worker	9. florist	15. nurse	21. veterinarian
4. chef/cook	10. firefighter	16. painter	22. waitress
5. computer operator	11. grocer	17. police officer	
6. dentist	12. janitor	18. pilot	

2. **BINGO, LOTTO, AND MEMORY MATCH GAMES** can easily be created with the photo cards. Use the reproducible Lotto game board *(page 88)* and the Bingo game card *(page 89)* to make the games. Complete directions for all three games are found on page 87.

3. **SNAP:** This is a fun game for 3 to 6 players. Copy two sets of the "People in the Neighborhood" photo cards. Shuffle the cards and pass out all the cards to the players. The first player puts down a card and says the name of the career represented by the person on the card. The next child does the same thing. Eventually two identical cards will be placed on the pile. As soon as this happens the students race to slam the card pile and yell "snap!" The last child to slam the pile has to pick up the entire pile and add it to their existing hand of cards. The objective of the game is to be the first player to get rid of all their cards.

4. **PHOTO FUN:** A great way to practice adjectives is to have the children describe people. The included photo cards can be used, or you may also have the children cut out pictures of people from magazines and catalogs. One at a time the children can show their picture to the class. Ask the child to describe the picture. Encourage responses such as; how old is this person; what type of job does this person have; and what might this person do for fun.

5. **WHAT DO YOU WANT TO BE WHEN YOU GROW UP?:** Make a classroom book about what the children would like to be when they grow up. The teacher should write on top of each page: "My name is _____ . I want to be a _____ when I grow up." Each child can illustrate their own page.

6. **GUESS WHAT I DO:** Pass out a photo card to each child. Have the children take turns describing the job or name some of tools that this person would need to perform their job. Have the other children guess what the person's job is.

7. **CHILDREN'S LITERATURE:** The following books will reinforce the career vocabulary:
   - Caseley, Judith. *On the Town: A Community Adventure.* Greenwillow Press. 1st Edition © 2002.
   - Kalmar, Bobbie and Walker, Niki. *Community Helpers from A to Z (Alphabasics).* Crabtree Publishing Company. © 1997.
   - Maynard, Christopher. *Jobs People Do.* DK Publishing, Inc. 1st Edition © 2001.
   - Rockwell, Anne. *Career Day.* HarperCollins. 1st Edition © 2000.

Photo Cards

Unit 14: School Tools

1. **REPRODUCIBLE PHOTO CARDS** are found on pages 67–68. *(English and Spanish Vocabulary Lists can be found on page 94.)*

PHOTO CARDS:

1. chalk	7. easel	13. notebook	19. pencils
2. chalkboard	8. globe	14. paint	20. push pin
3. clock	9. glue	15. paper	21. school books
4. colored chalk	10. lunchbox	16. paste	22. student desk
5. crayon	11. math test	17. pen	23. scissors
6. crayons	12. microscope	18. pencil	24. stapler

2. **BINGO, LOTTO, AND MEMORY MATCH GAMES** can easily be created with the photo cards. Use the reproducible Lotto game board *(page 88)* and the Bingo game card *(page 89)* to make the games. Complete directions for all three games are found on page 87.

3. **BACKPACK:** Directions for this reproducible activity are found on page 69.

4. **SURPRISE BOX:** Place a variety of classroom school tools in a box (pencils, crayons, markers, tape, paper clips, glue, ruler, paper, chalk, and scissors). One at a time, have the children close their eyes, put their hand into the box, and pull out an object. The children should be able to identify the object by simply touching it.

5. **LABEL IT:** This is an effective teaching method for any group of young children or children of any age who are being introduced to a new language and want to learn new vocabulary quickly. Simply label everything and anything you can in the classroom. You will be amazed at how many words the children learn to recognize in a relatively short amount of time.

6. **ART CENTER:** Organize an art learning center in your classroom. Help stimulate the children's imagination by providing an easel, paper, paints, playdough, crayons, glue, fabric, wrapping paper, and ribbon. The children will become familiar with using various art materials, increase fine motor skills, and build vocabulary as they experience all the different materials.

7. **CHILDREN'S LITERATURE:** The following books will reinforce school tools vocabulary:
   - Danneberg, Julie and Love, Judith DuFour. *First Day Jitters.* Charlesbridge Publishing, Inc. © 2000.
   - Kids Can Press, Ltd. *Franklin Goes to School.* Scholastic, Inc. © 1995.
   - Numeroff, Laura. *If You Take A Mouse to School.* Laura Geringer Books. © 2002.
   - Snyder, Inez. *School Tools.* Scholastic Library Publishing. © 2001.
   - Weiss, Ellen and Weiss, Leatie. *My Teacher Sleeps in School.* Puffin Books. © 1985.
   - Wiseman, B. *Morris Goes to School.* HarperCollins Publishers. © 1983.

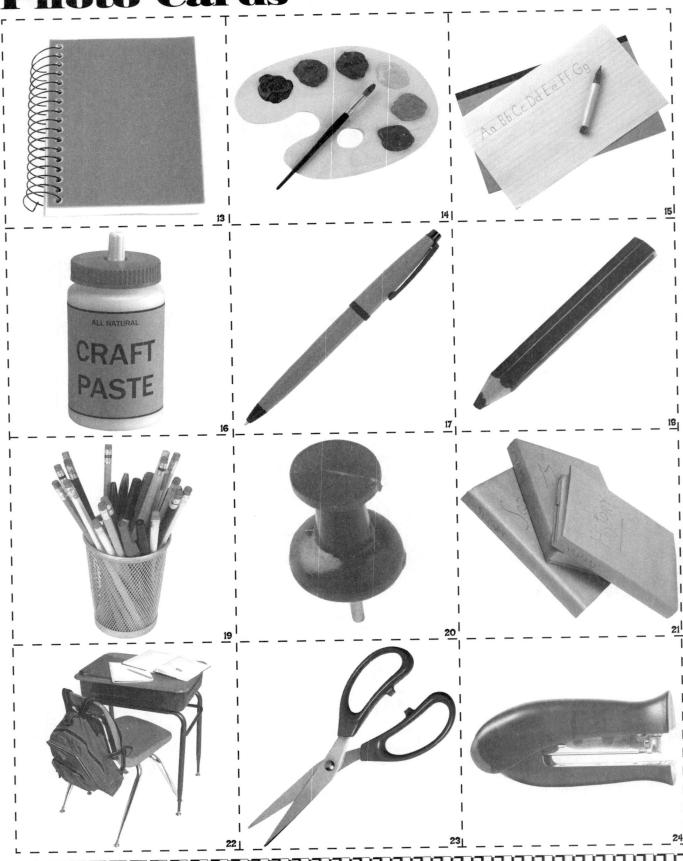

13

14

15

16

17

18

19

20

21

22

23

24

Backpack

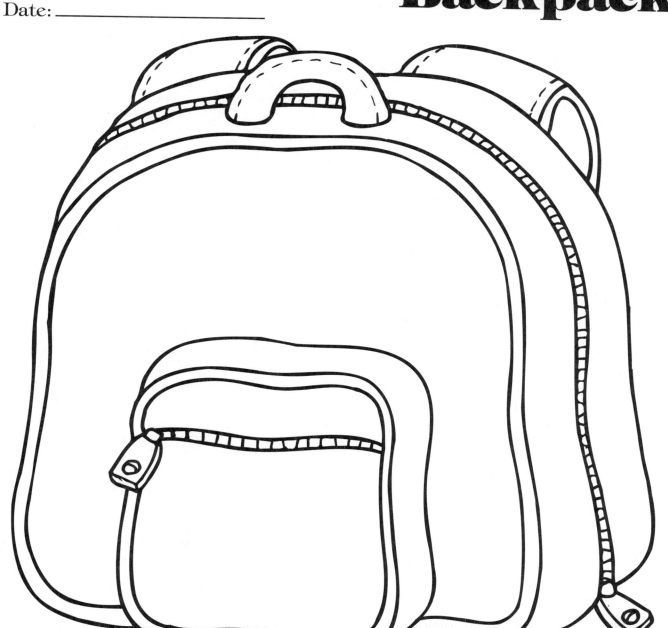

Directions: Cut the pictures out along the dotted lines. Glue onto the backpack. Name each object.

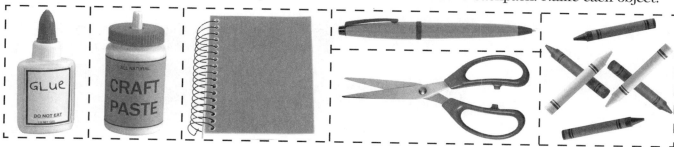

Unit 15: Shapes

1. **REPRODUCIBLE PHOTO CARDS** are found on pages 71–72. *(English and Spanish Vocabulary Lists can be found on page 94.)*

PHOTO CARDS:

(page 71)

1. circle
2. square
3. triangle
4. rectangle
5. oval
6. diamond
7. star
8. heart
9. octagon

(page 72)

1. circle/ball
2. square/dice
3. triangle/cone
4. rectangle/frame
5. oval/plate
6. diamond/kite
7. star/cookie cutter
8. heart/candy box
9. octagon/stop sign

2. **BINGO, LOTTO, AND MEMORY MATCH GAMES** can easily be created with the photo cards. Use the reproducible Lotto game board *(page 88)* and the Bingo game card *(page 89)* to make the games. Complete directions for all three games are found on page 87.

3. **SHAPE PHOTO CARDS:** Reproduce pages 71–72 for each child. The children should match the solid shape with the shape found in a real object.

4. **SPIN THE SHAPE:** Have all the children sit in a circle. Let the children take turns spinning a bottle. When the bottle stops spinning, the child the bottle is pointing to gets to pick up a shape photo card, tell the group what the shape is, and then gets to spin the bottle. Children think this is very fun and they will quickly learn the names of the shapes. This game can be played with all the units presented in this book.

5. **TIC-TAC-TOE:** Create a giant tic-tac-toe board (nine squares). Place a shape card face down in each section of the board. Divide the children into two teams. Students choose a card from the grid. If they know the shape, they get to place either a "X" or an "O" on that space. The team that gets three in a row (vertical, horizontal, or diagonal) wins the game.

6. **GIANT SHAPE MURAL:** The teacher should pre-cut a large variety of construction paper shapes. The children can then use these shapes to create a giant mural on a bulletin board or blackboard. The shapes can turn into flowers, houses, trees, cars, kites, and so many more things. Use pattern blocks as a guide for what shapes to cut.

7. **OVERHEAD PROJECTOR:** Place pattern blocks on the overhead projector and project them onto a large piece of paper. Let the children trace the shapes on the paper. The children will also enjoy deciding which shapes will be placed on the projector. After all the shapes are traced the children can either color or paint them.

8. **CHILDREN'S LITERATURE:** The following books will reinforce the shape vocabulary:
    *   Dorling Kindersley. *Touch & Feel Shapes.* Dorling Kindersley Publishing. 1st Edition © 2000.
    *   Hoban, Tana. *Shapes, Shapes, Shapes.* William Morrow & Company. © 1995
    *   Seuss, Dr. *The Shape of Me and Other Stuff.* Random House, Inc. Board Edition © 1997.

Photo Cards

1

2

3

4

5

6

7

8

9

Unit 16: Things Kids Do

1. **REPRODUCIBLE PHOTO CARDS** are found on pages 74–77. *(English and Spanish Vocabulary Lists can be found on pages 94–95.)*

PHOTO CARDS:
(page 74)

1. birthday party
2. riding the school bus
3. brushing teeth
4. practicing music lesson
5. playing at the beach
6. baking a cake

7. eating breakfast
8. collecting bugs
9. washing the car
10. playing with toys
11. playing chess
12. playing clapping games

(page 75)

13. coloring pictures
14. playing on a computer
15. playing with dolls
16. going fishing
17. playing football
18. talking with teacher

19. playing with parents
20. going to bed at night
21. doing homework
22. playing on the playground
23. playing with friends
24. making a lemonade stand

(page 76)

25. playing with marbles
26. painting
27. talking on the phone
28. taking care of your pets
29. playing with clay
30. playing baseball

31. reading in bed
32. reading at school
33. riding a bike
34. getting ready to roller blade
35. riding scooters
36. eating a snack or lunch

(page 77)

37. playing in the snow
38. playing soccer
39. playing in the sprinkler
40. studying at school
41. going swimming
42. swinging

43. watching television
44. getting into trouble
45. playing tennis
46. playing a video game

3. **THE NAME GAME:** This is a challenging game that can be a lot of fun. It requires that the children pay close attention to and listen carefully to what the other children are saying. The goal of the game is for the children to each say their own name and state something else about themselves. It will then be repeated by the other children. For example, the teacher could begin the game by saying, "My name is Mrs. Flora and I like dogs." The next child would say, "This is Mrs. Flora and she likes dogs. My name is Kari and I like flowers." The third child would say, "This is Mrs. Flora and she likes dogs. And this is Kari and she likes flowers. My name is Calleb, and I like to swim." The game keeps going until the list is just too long and there is too much information to remember.

2. **BINGO, LOTTO, AND MEMORY MATCH GAMES** can easily be created with the photo cards. Use the reproducible Lotto game board *(page 88)* and the Bingo game card *(page 89)* to make the games. Complete directions for all three games are found on page 87.

4. **CHILDREN'S LITERATURE:** The following books will reinforce the action vocabulary:
- Baer, Edith. *This is the Way We Go to School.* Scholastic, Inc. © 1990.
- Caseley, Judith. *Field Day Friday.* Greenwillow. © 2000.
- Dunn, Opal. *Acka Backa Boo!: Playground Games from Around the World.* Henry Holt & Company, Inc. © 2000.
- Falconer, Ian. *Olivia.* Simon & Schuster Children's Publishing. © 2000.
- Gollub, Matthew. *The Jazz Fly.* Tortuga Press. © 2000.
- Katz, Karen. *Excuse Me!: A Little Book of Manners.* Grosset & Dunlap: Liftflap Edition. © 2002.
- Lionni, Leo. *Let's Play.* Knoph Books for Young Readers. Board Edition © 2003.
- Yolen, Jane. *How Do Dinosaurs Clean Their Rooms.* Scholastic, Inc. © 2004.

25

26

27

28

29

30

31

32

33

34

35

36

Unit 17: Toys

1. **REPRODUCIBLE PHOTO CARDS** are found on pages 79–80. *(English and Spanish Vocabulary Lists can be found on page 95.)*

PHOTO CARDS:

(page 79)

1. airplane
2. baseball bat
3. basketball
4. bike
5. bubbles
6. doll
7. drum
8. Jack-in-the-box
9. kite
10. marbles
11. roller blades
12. rubber duck

(page 80)

13. shovel & pail
14. skateboard
15. sled
16. soccer ball
17. stick horse
18. teddy bear
19. top
20. train
21. tricycle
22. truck
23. wagon
24. wooden blocks

2. **BINGO, LOTTO, AND MEMORY MATCH GAMES** can easily be created with the photo cards. Use the reproducible Lotto game board *(page 88)* and the Bingo game card *(page 89)* to make the games. Complete directions for all three games are found on page 87.

3. **TOY BOX:** Directions for this reproducible activity are found on page 81.

4. **HIDE A TOY:** Show the children a small toy and tell them to take a good look at it because you are now going to hide it somewhere in the classroom. Once the toy is hidden, choose two children to search for the toy. Guide their search by using such words as "near" and "far" or "up" and "down." After you have played this game several times, let one of the children choose an object and then guide the "searchers" as they search for the object.

5. **I SPY SOMETHING:** This is a wonderful game for teaching prepositions. The teacher looks around the room and chooses a toy or some object that the children are familiar with. The teacher gives clues to help the children figure out what object the teacher is thinking about. Start the game by saying, "I spy something near the bookshelves." The children then begin guessing. (Use words such as near, by, next to, over, under, up, and down).

6. **TOY STORE:** Arrange a "toy store" learning center for the children. Provide shopping bags, a cash register, and shelves filled with toys. While the children are playing in the store, they will be using new vocabulary, practicing their math skills, and having fun socializing with the other children.

7. **CHILDREN'S LITERATURE:** The following books will reinforce the toy vocabulary:
   • Cronin, Doreen. *Diary of a Worm.* HarperCollins Publishers. © 2003.
   • Falconer, Ian. *Olivia . . . and the Missing Toy.* Simon & Schuster Children's Publishing. © 2003.
   • Freeman, Don. *Corduroy.* Puffin Books. Reprinted Edition © 1968.
   • Murphy, Stuart J. *Beep Beep, Vroom Vroom!* HarperCollins Children's Books. © 1999.
   • Piekart, Ferry. *Playing with Stuff: Outrageous Games with Ordinary Objects.* Kane/Miller Book Publishers. © 2004.

Photo Cards

13

14

15

16

17

18

19

20

21

22

23

24

Name:_____

Date:_____

Toy Box

Directions: Cut out the pictures of the toys and glue in the toy box. Encourage the children to name the toys. The children can also look through magazines and catalogs for other pictures of toys to add to the toy box.

TOYS

Unit 18: Verbs

1. **REPRODUCIBLE PHOTO CARDS** are found on pages 83–86. *(English and Spanish Vocabulary Lists can be found on page 95.)*

PHOTO CARDS:

(page 83)

1. bathing
2. batting
3. blowing bubbles
4. building
5. camping
6. climbing
7. coloring
8. crawling
9. crying
10. dancing
11. drinking
12. eating

(page 84)

13. feeding
14. fishing
15. floating
16. flying a kite
17. gardening
18. hugging
19. kissing
20. laughing
21. listening
22. looking
23. painting
24. peeking

(page 85)

25. playing
26. raising a hand
27. raking
28. reading
29. riding a bike
30. running
31. sitting
32. skating
33. skipping
34. sleeping
35. smelling
36. smiling

(page 86)

37. splashing
38. swimming
39. swinging
40. talking
41. thinking
42. tickling
43. walking
44. waving
45. working
46. writing

2. **BINGO, LOTTO, AND MEMORY MATCH GAMES** can easily be created with the photo cards. Use the reproducible Lotto game board *(page 88)* and the Bingo game card *(page 89)* to make the games. Complete directions for all three games are found on page 87.

3. **ACTION RACE:** This is an exciting relay race game that will delight the children. Divide the children into two or more teams and have the teams line up at one end of the room. The teacher will use words such as hop, crawl, skip, jump, walk, run, or tip-toe to tell the children how to move during the race. The children must follow that direction and move to the other side of the room, turn around, return to the next student in line, and then go to the end of the line. Once the child is at the end of the line the next player begins. The trick of the game is that the teacher can change the manner of movement at any time. Whenever the children hear a new direction they must change the way they are moving.

4. **CHARADES WITH VERBS:** Place all the verb photo cards face down. One child at a time picks a card and then acts out the action. The student who guesses the correct action is the next child to choose a card.

5. **CHILDREN'S LITERATURE:** The following books will reinforce the verb vocabulary:
   * Berger, Terry et all. *Ben's ABC Day.* William Morrow & Company Library. © 1982.
   * Gundersheim, Karen. *ABC, Say with Me.* HarperCollins Publishers. © 1984.
   * Hood, Christine. *Just Like Me (Learn to Read, Read to Learn).* Rebound by Sagebrush. © 1996.
   * Kent, Jack. *Jack Kent's Hop, Skip, and Jump Book: An Action Word Book.* Random House. © 1974.
   * Maestro, Betsy. *Busy Book of Action Words.* Random House Value Publishing. © 1988.
   * Noll, Sally. *Jiggle, Wiggle, Prance.* Puffin Books. Reprint Edition © 1993.

Photo Cards

Photo Cards

Verbs

Photo Cards

Photo Cards

Directions for Bingo, Lotto, & Memory Match

PHOTO CARD BINGO

What you need: Photo cards from any of the units in this book; pennies or small pieces of construction paper to be used as markers; the reproducible bingo card pattern found on page 89; scissors; and glue.

How to make the game: Copy the bingo game card onto card stock. Make as many game cards as you have players. Copy enough photo cards *(at a 50% reduction)* to fill each section of all the bingo cards. Cut out the photos, tape or glue them in each section, and laminate for durability. Make sure that you vary the arrangement of the photos on each bingo card. Store the bingo cards in a file folder. Attach a small resealable plastic bag to the inside of the file folder for storing the markers and calling cards. Copy an additional set of photo cards to be used as the calling cards.

How to play: Choose a child to be the caller and then pass out bingo game cards to each player. Remind the players to put a marker on the "free" space. The caller begins the game by drawing a card and in a clear voice, says the name of the photo. The players cover that photo with a marker. The game continues until one child has five markers in a row—either horizontally, vertically, or diagonally.

Variation: The game can also be won in three other ways: when a player covers the four corners; creates a "T" by covering the top horizontal row and the middle vertical row; or by creating an "L" by covering the first vertical row and the bottom horizontal row. It is fun to have a basket of small prizes *(stickers or bookmarks)* to reward the winners.

PHOTO CARD LOTTO

What you need: Photo cards from any of the units in this book; the reproducible lotto card pattern found on page 88; scissors; and glue.

How to make the game: Copy the lotto game cards onto card stock. Make as many cards as you have players. Copy enough photo cards *(at a 75% reduction)* to fill each section on all the lotto cards. Cut out the photos, tape or glue them in each section, and laminate for durability. Make sure that you vary the arrangement of the photos on each lotto game card. Store the photo lotto game in a file folder just like the bingo game.

How to play: (2 to 6 players) Give each child a lotto game card and place a deck of photo cards on the table. You should reproduce the same number of photo cards as the number of children playing. Each child takes a turn drawing a card. If the drawn card matches a photo on the lotto game card, the child gets to keep that photo card. If the child draws a card that they already have—that card is then returned to the bottom of the deck and the next child draws a card. The first child to have matched all twelve photos on the game card is the winner. This can also be used in a learning center as an independent sorting activity.

PHOTO CARD MEMORY MATCH

How to make the game: Copy two sets of photo cards onto card stock. Laminate for durability.

How to play: Decide how many pairs of cards you will be using—keeping in mind that younger children may be overwhelmed if too many pairs are used. Randomly lay the cards face down. The first player turns over two cards, searching for a match. If the cards match, the player gets to keep them. If the cards do not match, they are turned face down again, and the play passes to the next player. The game continues until all the cards have been matched. The player with the most cards wins! Remember to encourage the children to name the photos as they turn them over!

PHOTO CARD LOTTO

LOTTO FUN

_____

PHOTO CARD BINGO

B	I	N	G	O
		FREE		

English – Spanish Vocabulary Lists

1 – ANIMALS
(Farm & Pets)
animals – los animales
cat – el gato
cow – la vaca
dog – el perro
duck – el pato
fish – el pez
hamster – el hámster
hen – la gallina
horse – el caballo
mouse – el ratón
pig – el cerdo
rabbit – el conejo
sheep – el borrego

(Wild Animals)
alligator – el caimán
elephant – el elefante
giraffe – la jirafa
hippopotomus – hippopotomus
(same in English & Spanish)
leopard – el leopardo
lion – el león
monkey – el mono
rhinoceros – el rinoceronte
shark – el tiburón
snake – la culebra
tiger – el tigre
zebra – la cebra

2 – BODY PARTS
ankle – el tobillo
arm – el brazo
back – la espalda
cheek – la mejilla
chest – el pecho
chin – la barbilla
ear (outer) – la oreja
elbow – el codo
eye – el ojo
finger – el dedo
foot – el pie
forehead – la frente
hair – el pelo
hand – la mano
head – la cabeza
knee – la rodilla
leg – la pierna
mouth – la boca
neck – el cuello
nose – la nariz
shoulder – el hombro
teeth – los dientes
thumb – el pulgar
toe – el dedo del pie

3 – CLOTHING
boots – las botas
belt – el cinturón
cap – la gorra
dress – el vestido
hat – el sombrero
jacket – la chaqueta – la chamarra
pants – los pantalones
purse – la bolsa
shoes – los zapatos
shirt – la camisa
socks – los calcetines
underwear – la ropa interior

4 – COLORS
black – negro
blue – azul
brown – café
color – el color
green – verde
grey – gris
orange – anaranjado
pink – rosado
purple – morado
red – rojo
yellow – amarillo
white – blanco

5 – DAYS OF THE WEEK
Sunday – domingo
Monday – lunes
Tuesday – martes
Wednesday – miércoles
Thursday – jueves
Friday – viernes
Saturday – sábado

MONTHS OF THE YEAR
January – enero
February – febrero
March – marzo
April – abril
May – mayo
June – junio
July – julio
August – agosto
September – septiembre
October – octubre
November – noviembre
December – diciembre

6 – EMOTIONS
angry – enojado
bored – aburrido
excited – enthusiasmado
grouchy – malhumorado
happy – feliz
sad – triste
scared – asustado
serious – serio
shy – tímido
silly – divertido
surprised – sorprendido
tired – cansado

7 – FAMILY/PEOPLE
baby – el bebé
boy – el niño
brother – el hermano
daughter – la hija
family – la familia
father – el padre
friends – los amigos
girl – la niña
granddaughter – la nieta
grandfather – el abuelo
grandmother – la abuela
grandparents – los abuelos
grandson – el nieto
man – el hombre
mother – la madre
sister – la hermana
son – el hijo
woman – la mujer

8 – FURNITURE
bed – la cama
bookshelves – la estantería
chair – la silla
clock – el reloj
desk – el escritorio
lamp – la lámpara
mirror – el espejo
sofa – el sofá
stool – el taburete
table – la mesa
telephone – el teléfono
television – el televisor

9 – EVERYDAY OBJECTS (house)
bathtub – la bañera
books – los libros
broom – la escoba
camera – la cámara
car – el carro
comb – el peine
computer – la computadora
cup – la taza
eye glasses – las gafas – los lentes – los anteojos
fan – el ventilador
flowers – las flores
fork – el tenedor
glass – el vaso
hairdryer – el secador
house – la casa

iron – la plancha
keys – las llaves
knife – el cuchillo
pan – la sartén
pillow – la almohada
plate – el plato
refrigerator – la nevera – el refrigerador
silverware – los cubiertos
sink – el lavabo
shower– la ducha
soap – el jabón
spoon – la cuchara
stove – la estufa
toaster – la tostadora
toilet – el escusado – el inodoro
toilet paper – el papel de baño –
            papel higiénico
toothbrushes – los cepillos de dientes
toothpaste – la pasta de dientes
towel – la toalla
vacuum – la aspiradora
window – la ventana

10– FOOD
apple – la manzana
asparagus – los espárragos
bananas – los plátanos
bread – el pan
broccoli – el brócoli
butter – la mantequilla
cake – la torta
carrots – las zanahorias
cauliflower – la coliflor
celery – el apio
cereal – el cereal
cheese – el queso
chicken – el pollo
coffee – el café
cookies – las galletas
corn – el maíz
doughnut – la rosquilla
eggs – los huevos
fish – el pescado
french fries – las papas fritas
grapes – las uvas

grapefruit – la toronja – el pomelo
green beans – las habichuelas – las judías
            – los ejotes
hamburger – la hamburguesa
hot dog – el perro caliente
ice cream – el helado
lemon or lime – el limón
milk – la leche
muffin – el panecillo
mushrooms – las setas – los champiñones
orange juice – el jugo de naranja
oranges – las naranjas
pancakes – los panqueques
pears – las peras
pie – el pastel
pineapple – la piña
popcorn – las palomitas de maíz
potato – la papa
pretzel – el pretzel
salad – la ensalada
sandwich – el sandwich
spaghetti – los espaguetis
strawberries – las fresas
taco – el taco
tomato – el tomate
waffle – el wafel
water – el agua
watermelon – la sandía

11 – NUMBERS
zero – cero
one – uno
two – dos
three – tres
four – cuatro
five – cinco
six – seis
seven – siete
eight – ocho
nine – nueve
ten – diez
eleven – once
twelve – doce
thirteen – trece
fourteen – catorce

fifteen – quince
sixteen – dieciséis
seventeen – diecisiete
eighteen – dieciocho
nineteen – diecinueve
twenty – veinte
twenty-one – veintiuno
twenty-two – veintidós
twenty-three – veintitrés
twenty-four – veinticuatro
twenty-five – veinticinco
twenty-six – veintiséis
twenty-seven – veintisiete
twenty-eight – veintiocho
twenty-nine – veintinueve
thirty – treinta
thirty-one – treinta y uno
thirty-two – treinta y dos
thirty-three – treinta y tres
thirty-four – treinta y cuatro
thirty-five – treinta y cinco
thirty-six – treinta y seis
thirty-seven – treinta y siete
thirty-eight – treinta y ocho
thirty-nine – treinta y nueve
forty – cuarenta
fifty – cincuenta
sixty – sesenta
seventy – setenta
eighty – ochenta
ninety – noventa
hundred – cien
two hundred – doscientos
three hundred – trescientos
four hundred – cuatrocientos
five hundred – quinientos
six hundred – seiscientos
seven hundred – setecientos
eight hundred – ochocientos
nine hundred – novecientos
thousand – mil
million – millón

12 – OPPOSITES

front / back – adelante / atrás
young / old – joven / vieja
awake / asleep – despierta / dormida
big / little – grande / pequeño
cold / hot – frío / caliente
happy / sad – feliz / triste
in / out – adentro / afuera
clean / dirty – limpios / sucios
man / woman – hombre / mujer
winter / summer – invierno / verano
few / many – pocos / muchos
fast / slow – rápido / lento
girl / boy – niña / niño
dry / wet – seco / mojado
near / far – cerca / lejos
tall / short – alto / bajo
night / day – noche / día
full / empty – lleno / vacío
closed / open – cerrado / abierto
loud / quiet – ruidoso / callado
on / off – encendido / apagado
hard / soft – duro / suave
new / old – nuevos / viejos

13 – PEOPLE IN MY NEIGHBORHOOD

baker – panadera
business people – negociantes
construction worker – albañil
chef/cook – cocinero
computer operator – operadora de
                    computadora
dentist – dentista
doctor – doctora
delivery person – mensajero
florist – florista
firefighter – bombero
grocer – tendero
janitor – conserje
librarian – bibliotecaria
mail carrier – cartero
nurse – enfermera
painter – pintor
police officer – policía
pilot – piloto

seamstress – costurera
teacher – maestro
veterinarian –veterinario
waitress – mesero

14 – SCHOOL TOOLS
chalk – la tiza
chalkboard – el pizarrón
clock – el reloj
colored chalk – la tiza de colores
crayon – el crayón
crayons – los crayones
easel – el caballete
globe – el globo terráqueo
glue – el pegamento
lunchbox – la lonchera
math test – el examen de matemáticas
microscope – el microscopio
notebook – el cuaderno
paint – la pintura
paper – el papel
paste – el engrudo
pen – el bolígrafo
pens – los bolígrafos
pencil – el lápiz
pencils – los lápices
push pin – la tachuela
school books – los libros de texto
student desk – el pupitre
scissors – las tijeras
stapler – la engrapadora

15 – SHAPES
circle – el círculo
diamond – el diamante
heart – el corazón
octagon – el octágono
oval – el óvalo
rectangle – el rectángulo
shapes – las formas
square – el cuadrado
star – la estrella
triangle – el triángulo

16 – THINGS KIDS DO
baking a cake – hornear un pastel
birthday party – fiesta de cumpleaños
brushing teeth – lavarse los dientes
collecting bugs – coleccionar insectos
coloring pictures – colorear
doing homework – hacer la tarea
eating a snack or lunch – comer un
                        bocadillo o almorzar
eating breakfast – desayunar
getting into trouble – meterse en
                        problemas
getting ready to roller blade – prepararse
                        para patinar
going fishing – pescar
going swimming – ir a nadar
going to bed at night – acostarste en la
                        noche
lemonade stand – vender limonada
painting – pintar
playing a video game – jugar juegos de
                        video
playing at the beach – jugar en la playa
playing baseball – jugar béisbol
playing chess – jugar ajedrez
playing clapping games – jugar a las
                        palmadas
playing football – jugar fútbol americano
playing in the snow – jugar en la nieve
playing in the sprinkler – jugar con el
                        rociador para el césped
playing on a computer – jugar en la
                        computadora
playing on the playground – jugar en el
                        parque
playing with clay – jugar con plastilina
playing with dolls – jugar a las muñecas
playing soccer – jugar fútbol
playing with friends – jugar con amigos
playing with marbles – jugar a las canicas
playing with parents – jugar con tus papás
playing tennis – jugar tenis
playing with toys – jugar con los juguetes
practicing a music lesson – practicar la
                        lección de música
reading at school – leer en la escuela

reading in bed – leer en la cama
riding a bike – ir en bicicleta
riding scooters – ir en patineta
riding the school bus – montar en
                    autobús escolar
studying at school – estudiar en la escuela
swinging – columpiarse
taking care of your pet – cuidar a tu mascota
talking on the phone – hablar por teléfono
talking with your teacher – hablar con la
                    maestra
washing the car – lavar el auto
watching television – ver televisión

17 – TOYS
airplane – el avión
baseball bat – el bate de béisbol
basketball – la pelota de baloncesto
bike – la bicicleta
bubbles – las burbujas
doll – la muñeca
drum – el tambor
jack-in-the-box – la caja sorpresa
kite – el papalote
marbles – las canicas
roller blades – los patines
rubber duck – el patito de hule
shovel and pail – la pala y la cubeta
skateboard – el monopatín
sled – el trineo
soccer ball – el balón de fútbol
stick horse – el caballito de palo
teddy bear – el osito de peluche
top – el trompo
train – el tren
tricycle – el triciclo
truck – el camión
wagon – el carro
wooden blocks – los bloques de madera

18 – VERBS
bathing – bañarse
batting – batear
blowing bubbles – hacer burbujas

building – construir
camping – acampar
climbing – trepar
coloring – colorear
crawling – gatear
crying – llorar
dancing – bailar
drinking – beber
eating – comer
feeding – alimentar
fishing – pescar
floating – flotar
flying a kite – volar un papalote o una
                    cometa
gardening – trabajar en el jardín
hugging – abrazar
kissing – besar
laughing – reír
listening – escuchar
looking – mirar
painting – pintar
peeking – espiar
playing – jugar
raising a hand – levantar la mano
raking – rastrillar
reading – leer
riding a bike – andar en bicicleta
running – correr
sitting – sentarse
skating – patinar
skipping – saltar
sleeping – dormir
smelling – oler
smiling – sonreír
splashing – salpicar
swimming – nadar
swinging – columpiarse
talking – hablar
thinking – pensar
tickling – hacer cosquillas
walking – caminar
waving – saludar
working – trabajar
writing – escribir

Awards and Incentives

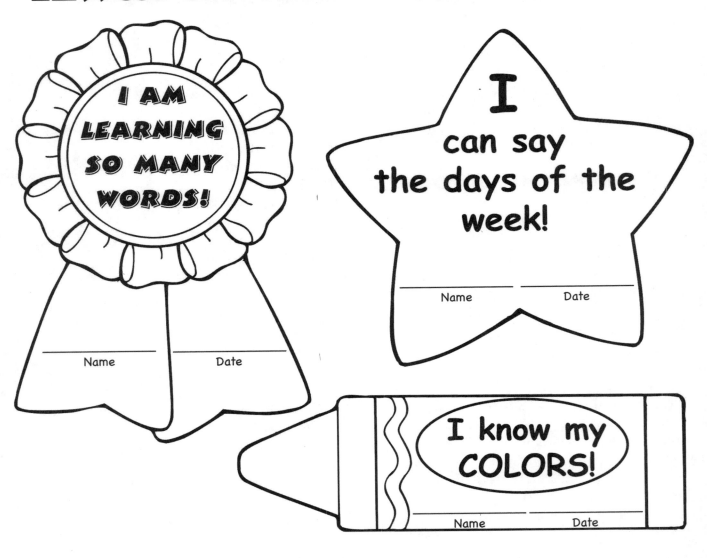

I AM LEARNING SO MANY WORDS!

Name _____ Date _____

I can say the days of the week!

Name _____ Date _____

I know my COLORS!

Name _____ Date _____

Date _____

I am bringing home new photo cards.

Ask me about them!

Name _____

I know _____ words!

Name _____

Date _____